All Types of Boats

By Sally Cowan

Contents

Float in a Boat

You can ride in all types of boats.

Some boats are slow,
and some are quick.

Boats float on streams, lakes and the sea.

Rowboats

You must row a rowboat, so it might be slow!

Speedboats

A speedboat is **very** quick.

It makes lots of foam.

Sailboats

The wind makes a sailboat go.

Without wind, a sailboat will not go!

This sailboat floats by the coast.

These sailboats line up in a row. Their sails are in a rainbow of shades.

Boats stop at a dock.

Throw a rope from the boat and tie it to the dock.

Ships

Ships are **big** boats.

They take big loads
a long way.

Ships roam the sea.

You can take a fun trip on a ship.

Can you see the small lifeboats?

Tugboats help ships get to the dock.

Strong tugboats tow and lead them.

My Boat

I can drive a boat!

I dip my toes in the lake and have fun.

CHECKING FOR MEANING

1. Which boat in the text might be slow? *(Literal)*
2. How do sailboats move? *(Literal)*
3. Why might it be difficult for big ships to get around at a busy dock? *(Inferential)*

EXTENDING VOCABULARY

row	The word *row* appears in the text with two different meanings. What are the two meanings of *row*?
loads	What does the word *loads* mean in the text? What other kind of transport carries a load?
tow	Read the word *tow*. What are the sounds in the word? What does it mean to tow something? What other word in the text sounds the same as *tows* but is spelled differently?

MOVING BEYOND THE TEXT

1. What is similar about the boats in the text? What is different?
2. Have you ever rowed in a rowboat? If you have, what was it like? If not, what do you think it would be like to row along a river?
3. What is your favourite type of boat? Why?
4. What kind of things might be carried in a ship's load?

TIME TO WRITE

Write about which of the boats in this book you would most like to ride in. Explain why.

PRACTICE WORDS

float

boat

boats

go

row

rowboat

slow

rowboats

so

coast

sailboats

speedboat

foam

toes

roam

rainbow

sailboat

floats

loads

low

throw

tugboats

lifeboats

tugboat

speedboats